# Luminous
## A 30-Day Journal

for Accepting Your Body, Honoring
Your Soul, and Finding Your Joy

Shannon K. Evans

**franciscan**
media®
Cincinnati, Ohio

Cover and book design by Mark Sullivan
Art on page 7: vecteezy.com
Copyright ©2021 Shannon Evans. All rights reserved.
ISBN 978-1-63253-388-3

Published by Franciscan Media
28 W. Liberty St.
Cincinnati, OH 45202
www.FranciscanMedia.org
Printed in the United States of America.
Printed on acid-free paper.

21 22 23 24 25    5 4 3 2 1

# contents

# how to use this journal

Your body is spiritual.

There are not two halves of you: soul versus body. You are one whole, made in the image of a God who is integrated and indivisible. Your relationship to your body cannot be separated from the health of your soul, for the two are intertwined to make up all that it means to be you. Your flesh and bones are sacred; they connect you to your soul's experience of the divine.

If you have chosen to embark on the journey of this guided journal, it is likely that you believe those words deep down and yet struggle to integrate them into your life in a meaningful way. Perhaps you have sought to love and accept your body for years, or perhaps this is a new venture for you. Either way, you are welcome. These pages can serve you well no matter your starting point.

As is true of all good inner work, you will get out of this journal what you put in. If you are not interested in going beyond the surface level, then these exercises will not likely change your life. On the other hand, if you are willing to courageously look at some of your deepest fears, wounds, desires, and questions, the next thirty days could be among the most transformative of your life. Remember, this is not a performance. No one is reading your words; this is a private exercise for you and you alone. The more honest and vulnerable you are willing to be, the more healing and growth can happen.

On a practical note, some women will enjoy the visual appeal of using colored pencils or fine-tipped colored markers on these pages. Other women will choose to keep it simple with a regular pen or pencil. All are great options. Flexibility is also available to you regarding the number of days you need: the journal is cued for thirty days of reflection, but only you know what pace is right for your lifestyle and needs. Perhaps you will require more than thirty days to go through these pages—perhaps less. There is no formula here, only an invitation.

One helpful hint: You are more likely to feel changed by this journal if you truly commit to it. Selecting a specific time of day can help you stay consistent in your inner work, perhaps first thing in the morning with a cup of coffee, during an afternoon break, or before going to bed at night. If possible, it's nice to have privacy in case strong emotions arise through the process.

And while the reflections and prompts were designed to be considered by you alone as an individual, you might like the idea of having another woman share the journey with you. In this case, you can buddy up with a friend, sister, mother, or even a small group of women who are going through their own copy of the journal at the same time. It might be encouraging to meet once a week and talk through the thoughts, emotions, and "aha moments" that arise as you journal.

Lastly, remember that this journal exists for you, not vice versa. If a given prompt doesn't serve your needs, feel free to follow the leading of your own soul that day; such listening will never steer you wrong. And above all, show kindness and compassion to your body in this process. She is doing a brave thing by asking you to love her.

*This journal does not provide expertise on eating disorders or other clinical diagnoses; neither is it a substitute for medical care or professional counseling. If your relationship with your body and/or food makes you feel unsafe, please contact your doctor to discuss your concerns.*

# part one

# Reconsidering

Imagine for a moment the sheer improbability of your even being here—of your body even existing at all. Your mother was born with one million eggs in her womb. Only about four hundred of those eggs would ever be ovulated during her years of reproduction. Your father released hundreds of millions of sperm cells at your conception. Think of it: The likelihood of your parents having formed you is astronomically small.

*your body is a miracle*

Now zoom out. Consider the odds that out of all the people on earth, the two who created you happened to cross paths at all, much less that their relationship would extend so far as to make a baby. Pause for a moment and appreciate your body for the marvel that it is. Some estimates put the likelihood of your existence at about one in four hundred trillion.

Science indicates that your body is composed partly of stardust. Faith tells us this was no accident. The presence of your body on this earth today is a miracle—a massive statistical improbability. And yet here you are, held fast in the divine generosity of this body you were given. Here you are, your flesh and bones a product of a perfect, generative, mysterious Love; a Love that holds all things together.

Here you are, a woman created for such a time as this.

*day one* On these pages, take some time to reflect on how unlikely your existence is—so unlikely it seems that it must have been ordained. Allow yourself the freedom to explore where these thoughts lead without judging yourself for the things that come up as you write.

*day two* The contemplative tradition centers on an awareness of the reality that all things are interconnected; all things find oneness within one another, and thereby within God.

With this contemplative posture in mind, think about the miracle of your body's existence on the planet, here against all odds. Let yourself be amazed and humbled. As you come to honor your place in the universal life of God, see if you can notice and physically feel the gratitude in your body.

The mandala is provided to offer you a physical way to move your body through prayer and free your mind to relish in a sense of awe and spiritual sensitivity. If you have colored pencils or markers, color the design in whatever way feels most reflective of your inner state. If you don't have such supplies, you can trace the mandala with your finger. The approach you use is up to you, but notice how you are engaging your body in the work of prayer.

# words matter

Think for a moment about the words you use to describe your body, both when talking to other people and privately to yourself. The words you speak over your body have power. Words can do violence, or words can nurture; words can wound, or words can heal. Whether vocalized or kept locked in your mind, your words wield serious power to direct your thoughts.

This doesn't mean you must use overly positive language that feels disingenuous to you; sometimes that's just too much to ask. Speaking in neutral terms about your body is fine, too. But the dominant cultural narrative is not neutral. It is written to make women despise and slander the very bodies that do so much for us. Countless industries make billions of dollars by keeping you dissatisfied or even disgusted with your own form. The more you hate your body, the more likely you are to spend money trying to change it. These industries' worst nightmare is a woman who joyfully accepts herself. They are playing a game of money and power; a game that cares nothing for you or the divine life that burns through your skin.

But what if you could change the narrative—if not for the culture at large, at least for yourself? And through that change, what if things could then change for your friends and daughters—maybe even for their friends and their daughters? What if you could write a narrative of being deeply and soulfully at home in yourself? What if you got to make the rules about what makes your body beautiful, what makes it worthy?

# *day three*

Take a moment to assess your current relationship with your body. In the space below, write down the specific words you have heard from others during your life about your body or bodies like yours. Which words do you personally use when you speak of or to your body?

Next, write down
your dreams for your
relationship with
your body. Not your
"dream body," but
the highest hope
you have for how
you could feel about
the body you're in
right now. If your
soul were completely
free, what would
it say about your
"today body"?

# day four

With acknowledgment that words carry power, make a list of all the good things your body allows you to do. These may be things like going for a hike, taking a bubble bath, giving birth to a child, making love with a partner, eating delicious food, or lifting an aging parent. Your answers are for you alone, so be as generous and as sensory as possible.

When you have exhausted your best ideas, sit back and read through this list as many times as you'd like. Then take a long, slow breath and say these words out loud, speaking to your body:

Thank you for making these small miracles possible.

We modern women are trained to distrust our bodies from a young age. Rather than being taught how to listen to and honor your body's messages with discernment, you have most likely been taught to seek mastery over your body through controlling things such as the amount of food consumed, the intensity of exercise, and your dress size. In some circles, this is even painted in religious language and made to seem pious— as though achieving dominance over your physical self indicates some kind of spiritual gift.

*Your Body Can Be Trusted*

But this mastery mindset separates the divinely intertwined parts of yourself. If you are seeking to dominate your body, there is no way to hear and trust the messages she is trying to send you. Your body is not something separate from you for you to control. Your brain was not created to dominate your body, but to live together in a harmonious relationship.

Trusting your body will teach you something about trusting yourself. When you practice deep listening within your body, you will begin to learn how to listen deeply to your truest self, too. Everything is connected. There is no separation within the parts of God's own self, and there need not be any separation in you, either. This is one mysterious way you embody the image of God.

*day five* Use these pages to reflect on the possibility of trusting your body. What has kept you from doing so in the past? How might it feel to accept the invitation? Tomorrow we will practice that trust, but for today, simply let yourself imagine the possibilities.

# *day six*

Spend some time in active listening to discern the messages your body is (and perhaps has long been) trying to tell you. You might notice immediate and practical things, such as hunger, aches and pains, or clothes that fit too tight; you also might notice more longstanding messages such as shame, control, and exhaustion. On the following pages, write or draw pictures of the words or sensations that come to mind. As you practice trusting your body to tell you the truth, remember not to judge yourself for what arises.

part two

# Growing

How does a woman measure her growth? Is it the weight she gained or lost? The mental or physical health she recovered? Is it finally accepting her small chest or big nose? These can be promising signs of life, but they don't corner the market on growth.

Growth also means letting go of control and judgment. Growth can mean changing your mind or expanding your worldview. For some, growth means saying yes. For others, growth means saying no.

*honor your growth*

How does a woman measure her growth? Only she can say.

Growth, both internal and external, reminds us that we were not meant to stay the same. You were meant to live a dynamic life that changes you for the better every step of the way. You were made to grow and stretch and take up space as you become a woman who knows what she has to offer the world. Do not fear becoming a softer, heavier, or more saggy version of your younger self; rather, fear the inability to see your own growth as good.

*day seven* Reflecting on the ways you have grown, take note of possible connections between the growth of your soul and the growth of your body. Perhaps your body has expanded in a way that feels true to your soul, or perhaps it feels like your body and soul are telling two different stories. Acknowledge and honor whichever experience is yours.

In the intuitive knowing of your soul, what divine invitation do you sense being extended to you? What work is necessary to find congruence between the growth of your body and soul? Remember that the voice of God is always affirming, compassionate, and tender. Refuse to listen to anything else.

# day eight

Claiming a mantra can help you find the "N" on your inner compass when you feel yourself getting off track on your journey of body acceptance. The sound of your own voice, coupled with the soothing nature of verbal repetition, sends messages to your brain that it is safe and affirmed.

Today, create a mantra to repeat aloud to yourself whenever you need a reminder that growing, changing, and taking up space are good and worthy things. Examples might include, "My outer change reflects my inner change," or "I am a human in constant process," or "I am worthy to take up space." Write your mantra and practice saying it out loud three to five times while breathing deeply. Notice the way your body begins to relax, even if ever so slightly.

Western civilization decided long ago that the ideal woman was small, convenient, and unobtrusive. Even with all our modern progress, women still hear the age-old message loud and clear: Don't take up too much space, literally or figuratively. Don't get any crazy ideas about deserving it.

# practice taking up space

And we do internalize these messages, no matter how badly we want to kick them to the curb. There are many ways women try to become smaller. There is diet and exercise, of course, but most of what we do is unconscious and harder to identify. Maybe you cross your arms and legs when you sit down—or maybe your habit is to pull a throw pillow over your lap. Maybe you squeeze into a size that became uncomfortable a long time ago. Perhaps for you, it's taking a flat iron to your wild, curly hair, or foregoing the fabulous heels that would make you "too" tall. Do you apologize when someone else bumps into you? Do you hesitate to speak up at work?

Men tend not to shy away from taking what they need spatially (we've all witnessed the "man sprawl" on airplanes or public transportation), but women are taught to fold in upon themselves. Yoga instructors who work with women often encourage them to practice wide, expansive poses every day specifically to practice taking up space— because so often, our souls heal through the movement of our bodies.

What if you took this challenge on as a spiritual practice? Perhaps you could try stretching out wide before you start your day or breaking the habit of always crossing your arms. Maybe you try letting your hair go wild and wavy or wearing heels that make you tower over everyone else. These do not sound like spiritual practices, but when done intentionally, they can communicate God's heart to you, reminding you that you do not exist to be a convenience to others. After all, this world is your world, too. You are entitled to take up space.

# day nine

Free write your own reflections on the pressure you feel to take up as little space as possible. In response, what are one or two simple things you can take up as spiritual practices?

*day ten* Make a list of the ways you have tried to make yourself smaller. Thinking outside the box, take note not just of the obvious ways but of the inner responses, motivations, and default settings that influence your way of being.

There is a pervasive, yet largely unspoken, lie that thin people are inherently more disciplined, more capable, and even more trustworthy than those with larger bodies, regardless of the facts. Have you bought into that lie? Is that the standard you have held for your own inner worth? Consider its subtleties. Many of us cognitively reject that belief, while still unconsciously internalizing it against our will.

*thinness does not equal worthiness*

The truth is that the size of your body has nothing to do with the condition of your soul, the ability of your mind, or the validity of your emotions. In many cases it doesn't even reflect the physical strength or fitness of your body. You can be a woman of any size and be perfectly qualified for the task at hand, physically, spiritually, mentally, or emotionally.
The only thing the shape of your body determines is the size clothing you buy— nothing more.

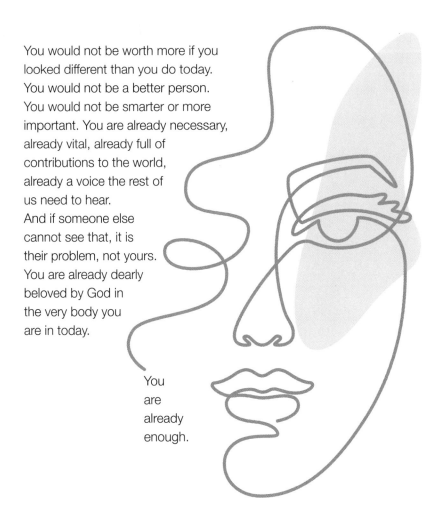

You would not be worth more if you
looked different than you do today.
You would not be a better person.
You would not be smarter or more
important. You are already necessary,
already vital, already full of
contributions to the world,
already a voice the rest of
us need to hear.
And if someone else
cannot see that, it is
their problem, not yours.
You are already dearly
beloved by God in
the very body you
are in today.

You
are
already
enough.

# day eleven

Write your own reflections on the temptation to equate your body size or shape with your value as a person. Where did you learn to connect those two things? How might you affirm yourself for your skills, abilities, and talents, exactly as you are?

# day twelve

Identify one specific lie you have believed about the relationship between your body and your worth. Use the blank page below to explore this more through drawing, writing, or any other medium that feels right to you.

# honoring the sacred nature of growth

Our bodies tell stories that we would often rather keep quiet. Whether it's cellulite, weight gain, stretch marks, stomach rolls, or big feet, our bodies tell the story of growth—the story of our rising and falling, our loving and losing. We are told we should be embarrassed about these signs of life; we are told to cover them up, make them disappear, or find any solution other than accepting them. But what if we decided not to?

What if, instead of being ashamed that those pants no longer fit, you affirmed yourself for the growth, maturity, and substance that you've gained since you last wore them? Not pretending that there is a direct correlation but letting what is visible remind you to see and honor what is invisible. Sure, maybe you went up a size since last year, but let that discovery remind you of the more important ways you have grown in that same amount of time. Maybe you took a big risk, got a job promotion, had a baby, learned about a justice issue, set an important boundary, deepened your faith, or cared for an aging parent. Look at all the important ways you have grown. Look at how much more these things matter than the inches around your waist.

The truth is that your relationship with your body can never be healed through diet and exercise—not in a real, lasting sense. There will always be something to dislike or criticize—always. Healing your body-soul connection has to come from touching on the sacredness of this vessel you inhabit. That means honoring the many ways your body leads you to develop, expand, and become more than you used to be. That means refusing to punish, restrict, and demean her. That means giving her room to flourish and grow.

# day thirteen

When you reflect on the inner growth and change that you have been most proud of in your life, what comes to mind? Free-write your thoughts and memories below.

*day fourteen* Identify one specific lie you have believed about the relationship between your body and your worth. Use the blank page below to explore this more through drawing, writing, or any other medium that feels right to you.

part three

Aging

Everywhere you turn, you will find anti-aging products for women. Nearly every beauty line for females has at least one product that makes such a claim. Men, on the other hand, are very rarely marketed to through such an angle. When a male movie star gets wrinkles and gray hair, he is called a silver fox. When his female co-star ages the same way, she is called washed up. We are all aware of this double standard, whether or not we consciously think about it. It affects us in ways both subtle and overt.

## aging and renewing

Having the gift of long years on this earth means that eventually our bodies will tell the story. Facial wrinkles, sagging body parts, varicose veins, liver spots, unusual moles, renegade body hair, stretch marks, cellulite, and gray hair are a natural and expected part of aging, not a reason for shame. Every human on earth has some combination on that list, and likely a few more. How you choose to manage (or not!) those things is up to you, but the invitation here is to find a kind of neutral acceptance rather than a strong emotional reaction to such bodily phenomena.

You can do this by reclaiming perspective. The more invested you become in the larger social and ecological landscape, the less likely you are to take your own aging too seriously. In a world where tragedy strikes left and right, the very experience of aging is a sheer gift; each day is one more opportunity for God to comfort and heal the world's pain through you. The years you have on this earth really are too short for all the goodness you wish to bring.

How are you using your years? Are you planting flowers, making art, engaging in activism, raising kind children, creating a more ethical workplace, or volunteering in your community? You are so much more than the lines on your face. Right here in this aging body of yours, you are creating, birthing, and building a better world.

# day fifteen

In the lines below, reflect on your own experience of aging.

# day sixteen

Part of the reality of aging is bearing witness to a long list of births and deaths—the reality of a constant tension between our gradual decay and our on-going generativity. Today, take some time to explore the births and deaths, both literal and metaphorical, that you have experienced or witnessed. How have they changed you? How have they invited you to live a more spiritually attuned life?

Births

Deaths

How many times have you heard a woman wistfully recall how small she was on her wedding day, graduation day, or other significant day of her life? Some women will even tell you how much they weighed at the time. Perhaps your mother reminisced this way. Perhaps you do.

# created to change

But consider this: Have you ever longed for the body you had when you were eleven? How about when you were three? Do you ever wish you were in your eighty-seven-year-old body today? The answer to these questions is most likely no. But truly, the longing to return to your sixteen-year-old body is equally as bemusing as longing for your six-year-old body. They were both good bodies for a moment in time, but you as a human being are constantly changing.

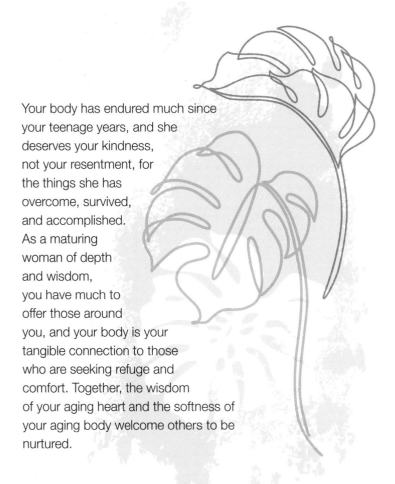

Your body has endured much since your teenage years, and she deserves your kindness, not your resentment, for the things she has overcome, survived, and accomplished. As a maturing woman of depth and wisdom, you have much to offer those around you, and your body is your tangible connection to those who are seeking refuge and comfort. Together, the wisdom of your aging heart and the softness of your aging body welcome others to be nurtured.

# day seventeen

In the lines below, free write your own reflections on how your body has changed throughout the course of your life.

# day eighteen

In four pictures, draw yourself at ages five, fifteen, forty-five, and seventy-five. What do you admire about each of these versions of you?

# Anti-Age Cream (a poem)

Just thirty-nine dollars a jar for the erasure of
each orbit around the sun.
One nickel to disappear every
iced tea on a summer patio, another for
singing in a blanket by the fire.
Three quarters for the week you sweated your way
through Malaysia, backpack at your hips.
One dollar to disremember sleeping in the bed
of a truck, another for sleeping beside the baby's crib.
Forty cents for the taste of honey between
lovers, sixty for the taste of forgiveness between
friends. A dime for every sleepless night,
eight pennies for the way the light hits your coffee cup.
How much for the time you folded your grief into a bottle,
set it out to sea?
How much for the ways you've learned to receive it back
again and again?

# day nineteen

In the lines below, write your own poem about aging. There is no right or wrong here; let it express how you truly feel.

# day twenty

Today, make a list of the things you like about getting older. These may have to do with your self-awareness, spirituality, worldview, hobbies, relationships, or any other area that comes to mind.

part four

# Peacemaking

Ours is a violent world. Physically violent, for sure, but violence is more than strictly physical harm. Violence is also cutting words, passive aggression, subtle injustices, power-grabbing, self-hate, and disregard for Creation, among other manifestations. Violence is anything that wounds and maligns a created being.

## peace starts within

Perhaps your body has experienced violence in your lifetime. Perhaps violence has been done to your mind or spirit with words about your body. These are tragedies that you neither caused nor deserved, trauma that merits deep counseling with a professional. Don't resist the help you need to live fully free in your one glorious life.

Not all of us have suffered violence at the hands of another person, but all of us have waged violence against our own body, mind, and spirit. Physical acts such as eating disorders or self-harm certainly count. So do acts of mental beratement, extreme dieting, verbal abuse, and comparing ourselves to other women.

The peace you desire to see in the world around you starts from within. And before you can make peace with your body, you must confess your violence against her. Is this some heavy emotional labor? Yes, but you can do it. Once you do, you can then forgive yourself. When you forgive yourself, you can make peace with yourself. And when you can make peace with yourself, you can begin to make peace all around you.

# day twenty-one

In the lines below, reflect on the ways you have done violence against your body in your lifetime.

# day twenty-two

What would it look like, in practical ways, to choose the way of peacemaking instead?

Much of our social structure is highly masculine. Historically, women have not been given much say in the formation of institutions like academia, religion, government, or even marriage. While great strides toward equality have been and continue to be made, women still find themselves in structures that were designed for male sensibilities and preferences. As a result, existing in these spheres can feel exhausting, frustrating, and isolating.

# embracing the feminine

The sacred feminine is needed. Although every woman reacts differently to the word feminine, in its purest form it represents something brazenly holy. The sacred feminine mirrors the part of the divine life that is inclusive, compassionate, resilient, and encompassing. It finds connection to God in earth and people above buildings and rules. It draws a wider circle so that no one is left outside the lines. It listens to the smallest voice and has no use for power games. It honors all but trusts the light within itself.

Whatever that ideal female body is that you can never measure up to, it's not God's design; it's man's. And somewhere deep inside, the God-within-you knows it. You do not have to pour yourself into a man-made mold in order to be worthy. The feminine wisdom in you knows that something more beautiful, more true, more whole exists. Whatever it takes, whatever it calls for, whatever you must do— find a way back to that Holy Voice.

# day twenty-three

In the lines below, reflect on your inner response to the word feminine. Explore the associations you have made with that word. What does it mean to you? What do you want it to mean?

# day twenty-four

What is the most affirming picture of femininity for you personally? Make a list of the things that evoke that feeling for you. Try to incorporate at least one of these things in your life every day.

# part five

# Connecting

When you see yourself as a part of the greater whole, you not only give greater honor to the whole, but you also gain a healthy perspective on your own significance. This is just one of the many gifts that Creation has to offer us. Growing a garden, taking meditative hikes, and increasing your environmental stewardship are all ways you can find your place within the whole. Getting your body, soul, and mind in tune with the natural world can have significant benefits to your quality of life.

# connected to the earth

You are not an isolated creature, not a mere accident tasked with going through life on your own. Your physical body is an integral and natural part of the planet you are on—one where your actions, attitudes, and even your thoughts impact the whole.

Stepping out into nature can remind you that you are not the center of the world. In relation to both the splendor and suffering of the earth, the way you feel about your physical appearance truly is a very small thing. You are part of something so much bigger—something so much better than the number on the tag of your pants.

Animals delight in their life without ever considering their shape or size. Plants do their work of photosynthesis without self-consciousness. Spending time in Creation—and finding your interconnectedness to it—invites you to stop taking yourself so seriously.

Step outside and let nature heal you. Appreciate the way your body connects you to the primal longing to belong— and belong here, you do.

# day twenty-five

In the lines below, free-write your own reflections about the connection between your body and the planet you live on.

# day twenty-six

Recall one specific memorable experience relating your body to the earth. Draw a picture or write about that time in the box below. What happened? How did you feel? What did you experience in your spirit that made this memorable?

Your body is magnificently yours alone, but it is also true that the people you love receive from your body in important ways. Your flesh and blood actually make life more comforting and less lonely for others. The wonder of being human is the endless domino effect of how our presence touches the hearts of others—often in ways we will never know.

## connected to others

When you hug a friend, make eye contact with a stranger, put a child on your lap, or caress a lover, you are opening yourself to allow God to communicate to another person through your body. We don't usually think of it that way, but if God is love, then that's exactly what is taking place. When your body communicates love to the world, it is acting as a vessel of God's Spirit.

Your body was given to you for your own pleasure, but it was also created for the good of others. Your body's power does not lie in how much it weighs or what shape it's in. Your body's power lies in its ability to offer presence and tenderness, both to you and to every human being with whom you are connected in this life.

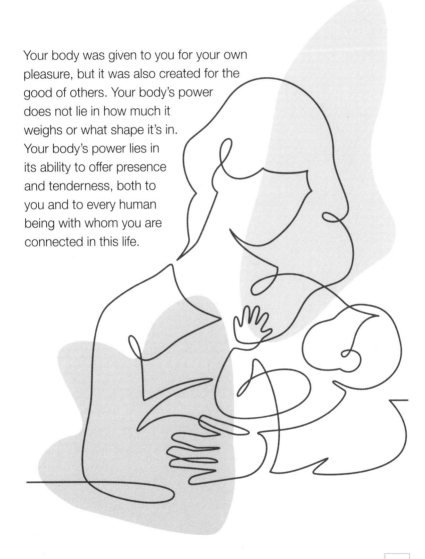

# day twenty-seven

In the lines below, reflect on the fact that your body connects you in deep and intrinsic ways to the bodies and lives of others. Explore your feelings about that.

# day twenty-eight

Think about your closest loved ones. What words might they use to describe your physical presence in their lives? Write those words on the lines below.

Your body is not an end in itself; rather, it offers the gift of tangible connection to the spiritual world. As a human, you experience God in and through your physical body. Perhaps this looks like kneeling and standing through your worship service. Perhaps it looks like singing or dancing. Perhaps for you it is hiking through the woods or meditating in the grass. The way you reach out for God might differ from the way of the next person, but you can be sure that if your heart desires divine encounters, then your body will put herself to good use to make them happen.

## connected to God

Have you ever thanked your body for this gift? For the fact that your limbs and senses help you organize your spiritual experience in a way that you can understand and recognize? When you consistently honor your body for this holy gift, it becomes harder to criticize and despise her. When you can feel the very life of God flowing in and through your body, connecting you to transcendence itself, it becomes easier to accept whatever shape she happens to take.

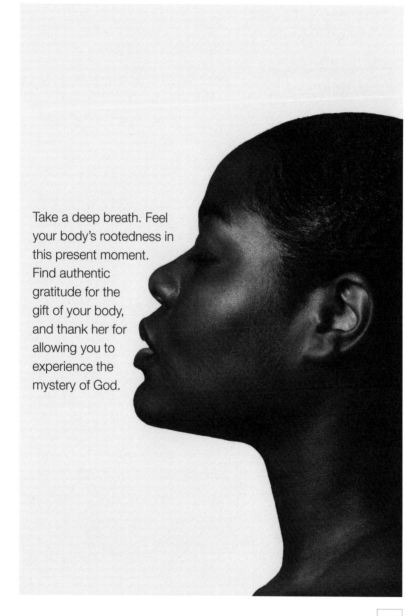

Take a deep breath. Feel your body's rootedness in this present moment. Find authentic gratitude for the gift of your body, and thank her for allowing you to experience the mystery of God.

# day twenty-nine

In the lines below, reflect on the ways your body connects you to God. How do you experience that connection with the divine?

# day thirty

Color the design below, and let the exercise lend itself to a prayerful meditation on weaving together your body and soul. You are a spiritual being. You are also a physical being. How do you desire to integrate those two parts of yourself?

You have now reached the end of your thirty-day intention to honor the integration of your body and soul. Perhaps you feel you have a different perspective on your body than you did when you began this guided journal experience, or perhaps you don't feel as differently about it at this point as you had hoped you would. Try to acknowledge and accept wherever you are in the present moment. In the work of body/soul integration, there is no "success" or "failure"—only a journey, with all its twists and turns. Having patience with yourself on that journey is a radical act of love.

As you move forward, take the parts of this journal that resonated most along with you. Revisit your favorite thoughts, continue practices you started, and keep using this book as a springboard to create your own prompts and spiritual exercises. Remember, your body was created for communion with God, and she is easiest to love when you engage her in your prayers.

May your future be filled with love, peace, curiosity, and joy. And may your body be filled with God. (Psst…it already is.)